SUPERHEROES

What is a superhero?
Find out by reading this fascinating
collection of more than thirty of your
favourite heroes and heroines. From
Asterix to Zorro, they're all here – complete
with facts about their origins, special
abilities, ambitions and enemies. No two
heroes are exactly alike, so you'll find
plenty of fantastic facts and feats to amaze
you, and there's even space for you to create
a superhero of your own.

SUPERHEROES

Gyles Brandreth
Illustrated by David Simonds

KNIGHT BOOKS
Hodder and Stoughton

Copyright © Gyles Brandreth 1984
Illustrations copyright © Hodder & Stoughton Ltd 1984

First published by Knight Books 1984

British Library C.I.P.

Brandreth, Gyles
  Superheroes.
  1. Heroes in literature—Juvenile
  literature   2. Heroines in literature—
  Juvenile literature   3. Literature, Modern
  —History and criticism—Juvenile
  literature
  I. Title
  809'.93352   PN56.5.H45

  ISBN 0-340-26808

Printed and bound in Great Britain for Hodder and
Stoughton Paperbacks, a division of Hodder and
Stoughton Ltd., Mill Road, Dunton Green, Sevenoaks,
Kent (Editorial Office: 47 Bedford Square, London, WC1 3DP)
by Cox and Wyman Ltd., Reading.

Contents

Introduction	7
My Superhero	9
Asterix	13
Batman and Robin	14
Biggles	17
Buck Rogers	20
Captain America	21
Captain Marvel	23
Dan Dare	25
Dr Who	27
The Fantastic Four	30
Flash Gordon	31
The Green Lantern	32
The Hardy Boys	35
The Incredible Hulk	37
Ivanhoe	39
James Bond	43
King Arthur	44
The Lone Ranger	50
Nancy Drew	51
Paddington Bear	53
Peter Pan	54
Popeye	57
Robin Hood	58

Robinson Crusoe 61
The Saint 65
The Scarlet Pimpernel 67
Sherlock Holmes 69
Spiderman 73
Superman 74
Supergirl 77
Tarzan 79
The Three Musketeers 82
Tin Tin 86
William Tell 87
Wonder Woman 90
Zorro 92

Introduction

This book is an A to Z of Superheroes. It includes all my favourites and I hope most of yours. It gives you the background to the lives and adventures of some of the most remarkable characters ever invented – and it tells you something too about the people who invented them.

On the whole, superheroes can be divided into two distinct types. There are those with their roots solidly fixed in science fiction, most of them American, and most of them beginning life as comic-strip cartoons. Interestingly enough, two of the earliest created are still the most popular: Flash Gordon (1934) and Superman (1938). And then there are the traditional superheroes, who rely on their own quick wits and strength of character to set them apart from ordinary mortals. While they do not have any magic or supernatural powers, characters such as Robin Hood and James Bond are still capable of great deeds of daring that cannot fail to impress us all.

While I was writing the book I tried to decide which of the superheroes I would most like to be and I kept changing my mind. Sometimes I wanted to be Sherlock Holmes, sometimes I wanted to be The Saint, but most often I wanted to be Superman. He is certainly the most famous of them all and he was invented by two seventeen-year-old boys from Ohio in the United States.

When you have finished the book perhaps you will be ready to invent a superhero of your own. If you do, you can fill in his or her details on the next page. Who knows, one day your superhero or heroine could be as famous as Superman or Wonder Woman.

Good luck!

My Superhero

What is his/her name? ....
....

When was he/she born? ....
....

Where was he/she born? ....
....

Who are his/her parents? ....
....

Where did he/she go to school?........................
....

Where does he/she live now? ....
....

When did his/her super powers first appear? ....
....

What are his/her super powers? ....
....

Does he/she have a special superhero's costume
and what does it look like?...............................
....

Does he/she have an 'ordinary' identity as well? ...
....

Does he/she have any special helpers or friends?...
....

Does he/she have any special enemies?.................
....

What has been his/her most exciting adventure so
far?..
....

Asterix

At the time when Ancient Rome is widening her territory and has conquered almost all of Gaul, in the far west of the country there is still one tiny pocket of resistance which stubbornly refuses to give in to the Roman invaders. This is the village where Asterix and his friends live. What makes them special? Why have they been able to hold out against the Romans when great chiefs like Vercingetorix have been defeated? The answer lies in a magic potion prepared by Getafix, the village druid. Getafix has a whole range of magic potions up his long white sleeve, but this particular one gives the drinker superhuman strength and Asterix and his friends take a swig whenever they need to teach the Romans a lesson. No one, apart from Getafix, knows exactly how the potion is made, except that it contains mistletoe, which Getafix gathers with a golden sickle, and lobster, which is added to make it taste better.

Asterix, a stubby little man with large hands and long flowing moustaches, can work his way through a Roman cohort like a mowing machine through dry grass.

Obelix, his gigantic friend, fell into the cauldron when he was a baby, and has had the strength of a giant ever since. He eats wild boar by the dozen and happily wanders about carrying huge stones, called menhirs, on his back.

13

Vitalstatistix, a fierce, red-headed warrior, is the tribe's chief.

Caconofix is the village bard.

The Romans have ringed the village with four fortified camps, packed with soldiers, and they have been struggling to conquer Asterix and his friends since 50 BC. They haven't got anywhere yet!

His origin

Asterix the Gaul was created by two Frenchmen, René Goscinny and Albert Uderzo and made his first appearance in 1961. In the past twenty years the stories have been published around the world and Asterix has appeared in cartoon films and on television. There is now a plan to build a huge *Asterixland* – like the American *Disneyland* – near Paris.

Batman and Robin

'Who are Batman and Robin?' the people of Gotham City ask themselves time and again, as the caped crusader and the boy wonder roar off into the distance after saving the city once more. They know that Batman and Robin fight crime in disguise, but no one knows their real identity. No one? Well, yes there is one person who does, but he will never let the secret out. Who is he? He's Alfred, a quiet, polite Englishman who works as a butler for a rich young man, Bruce Wayne, and his ward Dick Grayson.

In real life Bruce and Dick don't look anything like the Dynamic Duo. They live in a large mansion outside Gotham City and all they seem to do is to enjoy themselves. But Alfred knows that beneath this carefree appearance Bruce and Dick are two of the bravest and most fearless men alive.

Bruce Wayne was the victim of a terrible tragedy when he was still a boy: he saw both his parents gunned down in cold blood by a thief in the street. From that moment Bruce vowed that he would devote the rest of his life to fighting crime. Fortunately his father left him a large fortune and Bruce used this to help him develop his body and his mind until he had a brain like a computer and a body which could perform amazing feats of strength and speed.

When all this was done he still needed a secret identity to disguise himself, and while he was thinking what disguise to adopt, a huge black bat flew into the room where he was sitting and Bruce realised immediately what he should become – and that's how Batman, the weird figure of the night who fights crime in Gotham City came into being.

It wasn't long before he needed a companion to help him in his struggle for law and order, and, being an orphan himself, Bruce adopted Dick Grayson who was also an orphan. Dick was the son of two circus acrobats who had been killed by an evil criminal and the boy's circus experience had made him fit and tough enough to be Batman's partner.

Bruce and Dick live in Wayne Manor with Alfred. From the outside the building looks normal enough. But deep underground is Batman and Robin's headquarters: the Batcave. Here they keep their special vehicles, the Batmobile, the Batplane, the Batcopter and the Batboat, which speed them to the scenes of every crime. On another level in the cave there is a fully equipped laboratory, a computer and a variety of instruments to help them track down criminals. And in other parts of the cave there are workshops, changing-rooms and even a small Batmuseum where they keep the souvenirs of their battles against crime.

Batman and Robin may appear to arrive in Gotham City by chance at just the right moment, but in reality they usually get a call from Commissioner Gordon, the chief of police. At night-time he summons them by beaming a powerful searchlight into the sky, which outlines the silhouette of a huge bat. At other times he has a secret telephone in his desk which gives him a direct line to Batman.

So much for the goodies. What are Batman's criminal enemies like? They come in all shapes and sizes and their crimes are as evil as their appearance. Amongst the most wicked are the Joker, 'the clown prince of crime', who leaves his victims with a 'ghastly clown's grin – the sign of death from the Joker!'; the Penguin, who leads a gang of villains dressed in smart evening clothes swinging deadly umbrellas; the Riddler, a crazy criminal who gives clues about his next crime before he even attacks; and, of course, the fatal, feline, female, Catwoman – a desperate criminal who is secretly in love with Batman.

Their origin

Batman was created by the American comic book writer, Bob Kane, and he made his first appearance in *Detective Comics* in May 1939. A year later Robin joined him and they've been fighting crime together ever since. They've appeared in films and newspaper strips and in 1965 Adam West played Batman and Burt Ward, Robin, in a television series that ran for several years.

Biggles

Like a lot of young men who wanted to join in the fighting during the First World War, James Bigglesworth (Biggles to his friends), was a little too young. When he went to join up he was only just seventeen, so he lied about his age and said he was eighteen. Biggles was very keen to fly and only three months after enlisting in the Royal Flying Corps, he found himself in an aeroplane for the first time.

Biggles was quick to learn, even though his first

trip up happened by mistake – he'd got into the wrong plane with the wrong instructor. Very quickly Biggles found he was a born flier and he took to the air like a bird.

He didn't really look like a fighter. He was slightly under average height, with fair hair and hazel eyes, but there was something about the line of his mouth and the look in his eyes that showed he was determined and had an urge to succeed – and succeed he did. Within three weeks of his first flight, Biggles took a plane up solo. This also marked his first experience at getting lost! He actually made a forced landing in a field next to his aerodrome without realising where he was. Despite this early setback, after only a few days more training he was given his wings and sent off to France as a fully-trained pilot. Altogether he'd done a bare fifteen hours flying, dual and solo!

Following his distinguished career in the Royal Flying Corps, Biggles transferred to the newly formed Royal Air Force and saw action again in the Second World War. After this his flying experience broadened. As one of the most remarkable British pilots ever to take to the skies his services were snapped up by Interpol, the international police organisation, who recruited Biggles as a detective.

Using his skills as a pilot and a hunter in dog-fights, Biggles tracked down ruthless criminals in every corner of the globe, flying against every known hazard. Then, from working with Interpol, he switched to working with Scotland Yard and took on their gallery of villains.

Working alongside him through all his adventures, Biggles was supported by his companions, Ginger Hebblethwaite, Algy Lacey and Lord Bertie Lissie, and together they took part in over eighty adventures.

His origin

The man who created Biggles, Captain W. E. Johns, had been one of the original pilots in the R.F.C. himself, and he used many of his own flying experiences to bring realism and excitement to his many stories.

Buck Rogers

Buck Rogers is an American Air Force lieutenant who has been transported five hundred years into the future – when he discovers that America has been overrun by hordes of 'Red Mongols'. He has been fighting ever since! Helped by his pretty companion, Colonel Wilma Deering, Buck has battled with his mortal enemy, Killer Kane, on land, in space and in the sea.

As well as Wilma, Buck's lucky to have a scientific genius called Dr Huer on his side. Dr Huer has equipped Buck with death rays, disintegrating rays and space rockets to help him in his struggles with all his enemies – who include tiger-men from Mars, pirates from outer space and Killer Kane's devilish accomplice, Ardela Valmar.

His origin

Buck Rogers was the first science fiction strip cartoon ever produced in America and it was created by writer Phil Nowlan. Buck first appeared in January 1929 and that makes him the longest lasting science fiction hero of all time. Buck Rogers has featured in books, on radio, in films and most recently on television where Gil Gerard plays Buck; Erin Gray, Wilma; Tim O'Connor, Dr Huer; and Mel Blanc (the voice of Bugs Bunny) provides the voice behind Twiki, the cheeky, metallic robot.

Captain America

The time is 1941, the place America. Across the ocean Europe is gripped by war. America is not involved in the fighting yet, but even now the country's defences are being weakened by terrorists and spies who are blowing up important military stores and buildings. The country is scared. 'What will happen if America does join the war?' people ask. Luckily others have thought of that too, and in a top-secret laboratory, hidden behind a shabby junk shop, the answer is about to be revealed to the nation's top army chiefs.

The generals are sitting in the laboratory watching a skinny young man being given an injection of a new wonder drug. 'Observe this young man closely,' the scientist tells his audience as the new drug starts to take effect. 'Today he volunteered for army service and was refused because he was of unfit condition! His chance to serve his country seemed gone.'

As the generals watch, the skinny body in front of them begins to grow huge, powerful muscles. The power of the new drug surges through the young man forming millions of new cells at incredible speed. His brain develops just as fast and when the growing finishes the scientist stands beside a tall, muscular man with a brilliant mind, ready to take on any enemy.

Unfortunately, at this top-secret gathering there is a spy listening to the scientist as he tells the generals that America will soon have an army of men like the one he has just created. The spy realises the threat that such an army would pose and before anyone can stop him, he whips out a pistol and shoots the scientist dead. With another lightning move he shatters the only container of the new drug and the brilliant invention dies with its creator.

The spy starts shooting at the generals sitting beside him, but no sooner has he started firing than a powerful punch sends him reeling across the laboratory. In his fright the spy struggles to escape and gets entangled in the high voltage electric cables that are being used in the experiment. As he struggles the cables break and a huge electric current reduces him to a pile of ashes – Captain America has dealt with his first enemy agent.

Yes, the weedy young man who was transformed by the drug becomes Captain America, the challenger of spies and enemy agents throughout the war. In real life Captain America is an ordinary soldier in the US army – Private Steve Rogers – but as Captain America, Rogers, dressed in a red, white and blue costume that looks like the American flag, takes on America's hidden enemies single-handed.

His origins

Captain America was created by writer Joe Simon and by artist Jack Kirby. He was very popular during and just after the Second World War. For a while very little was heard of him, but after fifteen years absence (he was trapped in an iceberg!) he reappeared in 1968 and is still going strong.

Captain Marvel

Billy Batson started life like every other boy. It wasn't until he visited the wizard, Shazam, that Billy's life made a sudden change. Shazam, gave Billy the power to change himself into 'The world's mightiest man – powerful champion of justice – relentless enemy of evil – Captain Marvel'. What's more, the secret of his incredible power was simplicity itself – all he had to do was say 'Shazam!!!'

Just by uttering this one magic word Billy Batson would transform himself from a skinny schoolboy into a muscular superhero dressed in red and gold. Why 'Shazam'? The word is an acronym (a word made up from the initial letters of other words) the S stands for Solomon's wisdom; H is for Hercules's strength; A is for Atlas's stamina; Z is for Zeus's power; A is for Achilles' courage; and M is for Mercury's speed. Anyone who possessed the qualities of all these ancient gods and heroes couldn't help but be a superhero himself.

Billy wasn't the only member of the Marvel family. There was Mary Marvel, Captain Marvel Junior, Uncle Marvel, three Lieutenants Marvel and even a rabbit, Hoppy, the Marvel Bunny! Set against this formidable group were colourful villains like Mr Mind, an evil genius of a worm; Mr Tawney, the talking tiger; and Dr Sirvava, a mad scientist, whose family were the arch enemies of the Marvel family.

His origin

Captain Marvel was a worthy rival to Superman when he first appeared over forty years ago. In fact, his creators, writer Bill Parker and artist C. C. Beck, made him so successful that the publishers of the Superman stories took them to court on the grounds that Captain Marvel was borrowing ideas directly from Superman. After a long court battle Captain Marvel lost and went out of print – for several years, but not for ever. In the 1970s he appeared once more in a comic book suitably called *Shazam*.

Dan Dare

If you want to know who Dan Dare is, you can turn to the official biography and this is what it will tell you: 'Daniel MacGregor Dare, Col. O.U.N. Interplanet Space Fleet – awarded the Order of the United Nations for his leadership of the Venus Expedition of 1996. Born Feb. 5, 1967 – Manchester, Cambridge and Harvard – became Class 3 Space Pilot by the time he was twenty. Spent two years on Planetary Exploration Course on the moon – became Chief Pilot of the I.S.F. at 30. Hobbies: cricket, fencing, riding, painting and model-making.'

Well, so much for the official version. What is he like in the flesh? Dan Dare's a clean-cut space officer with eyebrows like jagged forks of lightning. He's a brave and brilliant pilot and a daring and dashing explorer, the sort of man who gets sent on the missions that no one else could manage – at least that's what his chief, Sir Hubert Gascoine Guest, would tell you if you wanted an honest answer. Dan's crew comprises 'Dig', officially

Albert Fitzwilliam Digby, Dan's batman and faithful companion; 'Hank', Pilot/Captain Henry Brennan Hogan, from Houston, Texas; and 'Pierre', Pilot/Major Pierre August Lafayette, from Dijon, France, who is quite as interested in enjoying good food and wine as he is in travelling in space. As well as Dan's official team he's frequently helped by Dig's Aunt Anastasia, who had a two-seater space-ship named after her, having played an important part in the overthrow of Dan Dare's greatest rival, the Mekon of Venus. The Mekon is a ghastly, green-skinned creature with a huge domed head. Dan Dare had him licked on Venus in 1996, but the Mekon managed to slip out of his grasp and lives on to plague the earth and our hero still.

His origin

Dan Dare was created at the same time as a brand new British comic, *Eagle*, which went on sale for the first time in April 1950. Dan's creator was a British illustrator, Frank Hampson, who taught himself to draw while he'd been working for the Post Office. From the front page of *Eagle* Dan Dare broadened out to his own radio programme and when the original *Eagle* came to an end he was revived with the Mekon in *2000 AD* and in a 1982 version of the *Eagle*.

Dr Who

The existence of Dr Who was first brought to light by a couple of school teachers. They'd noticed that one of the girls in their class had an extraordinary knowledge of history, far beyond that which they would have expected to find in someone of her age. This made them curious to discover more about her background and one afternoon they followed her home from school to find out where she lived. Their curiosity was aroused when they saw her disappear inside what looked like a police telephone-box, and they tiptoed in behind her. To their amazement they found that they hadn't walked into a police telephone-box at all, but into a time machine, the Tardis. What from the outside had looked a tiny phone-box had suddenly turned into a spacious vehicle filled with banks of weird-looking scientific instruments.

Inside the Tardis they also met the girl's grumpy old grandfather, Dr Who. He was a Time Lord, who travelled through time and space visiting different planets and different civilisations. For all his genius, however, Dr Who didn't have full control over the Tardis and while the two teachers were still inside it, the time machine suddenly started up and carried them back through time to the Stone Age!

After this first adventure Dr Who encountered perhaps his best known adversaries, the Daleks.

This race of gravel-voiced robots with revolving domed-heads and lethal ray-guns travelled about the Dead Planet finishing off their enemies with the words 'exterminate . . . exterminate' and a blast of deadly rays. Of course the Daleks are only one of the many strange groups that Dr Who and his companions have encountered in their travels. It is twenty years now since the two teachers first uncovered the doctor's secret and in that time he has visited a wide variety of different galaxies and ages with a number of different companions.

His origin

Dr Who made his first appearance on BBC television in November 1963 and his adventures now form the longest running science fiction series on T.V. Six different actors have played the part of Dr Who: the series began with William Hartnell; after him came Patrick Troughton; then there was Jon Pertwee (now the scarecrow in *Worzel Gummidge*); then came Tom Baker (famous for his curly hair and long woolly scarf), after that, Peter Davidson and now the part is being played by Colin Baker. Dr Who has also appeared in over forty novels and been the subject of two full-length feature films: *Dr Who and the Daleks* (1965) and *Daleks – Invasion Earth 2150 AD* (1966).

The Fantastic Four

The Fantastic Four are superheroes with a very human side to their personalities.

Mr Fantastic, Reed Richards in real life, is a brilliant scientist who can stretch his limbs to incredible length. Sadly, like all too many brilliant people, he can be thoughtless and unfeeling when dealing with others. His wife, Sue, is the Invisible Girl. She can make herself disappear whenever she chooses, but this doesn't prevent her sometimes from behaving in an immature and childish way. Then there's Sue's brother, Johnny Storm (The Human Torch), who's so quick-tempered that he literally bursts into flames at a moment's notice. Finally, the fourth of the Fantastic Four, is poor Ben Grimm (The Thing), who has all sorts of emotional problems due to his hideous appearance. Normally he's a tough, likeable guy, but when he changes into his superhero role, he turns into a monstrous, orange-coloured creature with incredible strength.

Lined up against the Fantastic Four are villains like Dr Doom, an eastern European monarch with even greater scientific powers than Reed Richards. He always appears in an iron mask to hide his badly scarred and damaged face. While on the side of the Fantastic Four working for peace and justice, are allies like The Silver Surfer, who is the next best thing to an angel on a surfboard.

Their origin
The Fantastic Four were created by American comic book writer, Stan Lee, and made their first appearance in November 1961. In the last twenty years they have become some of the most successful and popular superheroes ever created.

Flash Gordon

Flash Gordon began his space-age career after graduating from America's Yale University, where he'd become well-known as a star polo player. Setting off with his girlfriend, Dale Arden, and a crazy scientist, Dr Hans Zarkov, Flash travelled to the planet Mongo in a desperate attempt to save the earth from destruction. The emperor of Mongo, Ming the Merciless, had threatened to destroy the earth and the three adventurers were going to do their best to foil his wicked plan.

Once they'd arrived on Mongo – they travelled in Dr Zarkov's own spaceship – Flash Gordon and his colleagues became locked in deadly combat with Ming. For the next seven years they struggled against him and explored the whole of his strange planet in the process. They discovered Queen Undina's undersea kingdom. They visited the land of the tuskmen and Queen Fria's ice kingdom. And all the time they were drawing closer to the ultimate conflict between Flash Gordon and Ming himself.

In the course of their adventures the three humans were aided by Ming's daughter, Aura, and her husband, Barin, the King of Arboria, and it was thanks to them that Flash Gordon finally came face to face with the evil emperor of Mongo and defeated him.

After only a brief trip home to the planet Earth, the three were off to Mongo once more, this time to fight the tyrant Brazor. They had to cope with death rays and rocket ships, wild jungles and dangerous dinosaurs – to say nothing of hand-to-hand fighting – until eventually Flash and his friends triumphed on Mongo once more.

His origin

Flash Gordon first appeared in a newspaper cartoon strip in January 1934, drawn by American artist, Alex Raymond. Films followed and throughout the 1930s and 1940s there was also a Flash Gordon series on radio. The hero had his own television programme in the 1950s and in 1981 Flash Gordon returned to the cinema screen in a brand-new multi-million dollar film.

The Green Lantern

The story of the Green Lantern begins long, long ago in ancient China. A group of villagers was working in their fields one day when a meteor crashed to earth and split wide open. The villagers were terrified when they went to look at this strange rock from outer space and saw a pool of flaming, green liquid lying inside it. But they were even more terrified when they heard a mysterious voice speaking from the green flames. 'Three times shall I flame green!' it said. 'First – to bring death! Second – to bring life! Third to bring power.' Then, when the voice had died away, the flames disappeared and the green liquid started to turn solid, changing into a green metal.

The first warning from the voice in the green flames came true before long. The village lamp-maker took the green metal and used it to make a lamp. The other villagers were frightened that this would bring evil on the whole village and they killed him. But no sooner had he been killed than the lamp began to glow with a green light which filled the workshop until all the murderers fell down dead.

The second time the lamp glowed was many hundreds of years later in a lunatic asylum in America. The lamp was given to one of the patients who transformed it into a railway lantern and when he lit it for the first time the same strange, powerful green light started to shine from it. As it grew brighter the patient's mind cleared and he was sane again. The green lantern had brought 'life' to the sick man.

The third prophesy came true after a railway

accident. Alan Scott, a young engineer, was sitting in the cab of the engine as the train made its first run over a new bridge that his company had just built as part of a large government contract. Alan was holding the green lantern in his hand as the train went over the bridge and suddenly a deafening explosion destroyed the bridge and sent the train and all the engineers plunging to the floor of the canyon below. Everyone on the train was killed in the accident – everyone except for Alan Scott.

When he came round Alan found that he was still holding the green lantern and that the green light was now shining all over him. Suddenly the voice from the light told Alan that he was destined to inherit the power from the green light and instructed him to make a ring from the metal in the green lantern and to wear it always.

Alan Scott followed the instructions and when he had made the ring and put it on his finger he found he was able to perform any feat he wanted to. He found he could fly; could pass through a wall; could even resist bullets and other metal objects that were used to attack him. The only material against which he had no power was wood. Armed with these amazing powers Alan Scott – alias the Green Lantern – set out on a crusade against crime.

His origin

The Green Lantern was created by writer Bill Finger and artist Martin Dellon. He first appeared in the *All American* comic book in July 1940. In 1959 a new Green Lantern appeared. His name was Hal Gordon and he inherited many of the powers from Alan Scott, including his special green ring. However, Hal Gordon *could* cope with wood: his one problem was that he had no power over the colour yellow!

The Hardy Boys

Frank and Joe Hardy live at Bayport on the east coast of the USA. Their father, Fenton Hardy, runs a private detective agency and the boys have picked up most of their investigative skills from him. Mr Hardy frequently gets called away on top-secret business and while he's away the boys step into his shoes and carry on his work.

This has brought them up against a whole gallery of rogues, many of them distinguished by sinister physical features such as scars, very large noses and shaggy beards! But the boys are well equipped to take on all-comers. Frank, the older one, is tall and quick-witted, while his younger brother tends to be more impatient, but is a real live-wire when it comes to the action. The boys have got their own car and a boat nicknamed *Sleuth*. If they have to travel long distances they can also use their father's plane, since fortunately both of them have pilot's licences. They've got good friends to help them too. There's fat, friendly Chet

Morton, who's as interested in food as Frank and Joe are in crime and when it comes to slugging it out with the crooks, Biff Hooper, a powerful boxer, is usually around to help out.

In the course of their crime-fighting Frank and Joe have had to cope with every kind of hazard and disaster. They've been kidnapped, knocked unconscious, drugged and attacked by wild animals. But with their track record of successes to help them through, they always manage to come out on top no matter how tough the opposition.

Their origin

Although the author of all the Hardy Boys stories is given as Franklin W. Dixon, this is really a pen name used by the many different writers who have written the stories. The Hardy Boys were actually created by Edward L. Stratemeyer, who also created Nancy Drew. Stratemeyer wrote several of the stories himself, but they became so popular that he had to employ others to help him meet with the demand for new Hardy Boys adventures. The stories first appeared in the late 1920s and the television series starring Shaun Cassidy and Parker Stevenson began in 1977.

The Incredible Hulk

The Incredible Hulk came into being as the result of a serious accident. Before the accident the Hulk had been a normal American scientist called Dr Bruce Banner. Dr Banner had invented a very powerful gamma-ray bomb which was due to be tested for the first time at a secret test site. Unfortunately just as the signal was given to detonate the bomb Dr Banner saw someone walking across the test area. He knew that whoever it was would be killed by the blast and, leaving his own safe shelter, he ran to save the trespasser, a young man by the name of Rick Jones. The scientist managed to reach Jones in the nick of time, but the bomb exploded seconds later and caught Dr Banner with the full force of the gamma-rays, changing him into a huge, snarling grey-skinned monster – the Incredible Hulk.

Dr Banner didn't remain as the Incredible Hulk all the time. Like the famous character in Robert Louis Stevenson's horror story, *Dr Jekyll and Mr Hyde*, Dr Banner constantly changed his identity, regularly switching from the human scientist to the hideous Hulk and back again.

Unfortunately his terrifying appearance as the Hulk makes everyone believe that he is evil, whereas in fact he always works for good. At first the Hulk's only friend was the man he saved, Rick Jones, but later he teamed up with both Captain Marvel and Captain America. To add to his other difficulties, the Incredible Hulk/Dr Banner had trouble with his girlfriend, Betty Ross. At one stage, Betty left him for another man, Major Talbot, but then came back to the scientist. She couldn't really make up her mind which of the two men she loved best, so she kept coming and going between them.

But if Dr Banner had problems with Betty, the Incredible Hulk had even greater trouble with her father, Thunderbolt Ross, who was Dr Banner's boss in real life. Thunderbolt Ross was a general in the army and became the Incredible Hulk's greatest enemy.

His origin

The Incredible Hulk was created by Stan Lee, who also created the Fantastic Four, and made his first appearance in May 1962. In 1977 the Incredible Hulk appeared in a television film for the first time, with Bill Bixby in the title role. The film was so successful that a whole series of television films followed.

Ivanhoe

The story of Ivanhoe is a story of knights in shining armour, jousting tournaments and medieval chivalry. Ivanhoe, or to give him his correct title, Sir Wilfred of Ivanhoe, was the son of Cedric of Rotherwood, a Saxon nobleman, who lived in the twelfth century, during the reign of King Richard the Lionheart. (In fact Ivanhoe lived at the same time as Robin Hood, who comes later).

Ivanhoe had the misfortune to be disinherited

by his father on account of his love for the lovely lady Rowena, a Saxon heiress and his father's ward. Ivanhoe's father wanted Rowena to marry a powerful Saxon nobleman, so Ivanhoe left with King Richard to fight in the Crusades, where he won great glory and became one of the King's favourite knights.

After fighting in Palestine, Ivanhoe returned to England in disguise and went in secret to his father's house to see Rowena. Still in disguise, he then entered the great jousting tournament at Ashby, calling himself Desdichado (The Disinherited). Ivanhoe won the tournament – of course! – and received the victor's crown from his beloved Rowena. Unfortunately in the joust he had been wounded, so after the tournament he was taken to the house of a friend, a rich Jew called Isaac of York. There the wounded knight was nursed back to health by Isaac's beautiful daughter, Rebecca, who fell in love with the hero.

While Ivanhoe was being nursed by Rebecca, Rowena was being held captive by Maurice de Bracy, who had kidnapped her and made her a prisoner in the Tower of Torquilstone. He vowed he would not release her until she agreed to marry him.

Although Rebecca was passionately in love with Ivanhoe, she knew that their different religions would always prevent them from marrying, so she generously tried to win Rowena's release by offering a knight, Bois-Guilbert, any sum he demanded to help secure Rowena's freedom. Bois-Guilbert proved to be more interested in Rebecca herself and when she rejected his advances he took her before a religious court, where she was found guilty of being a witch and was condemned to death. Rebecca then asked Ivanhoe to be her champion in a trial by combat and when he won the fight, she was allowed to go free.

In the meantime King Richard returned to England and, disguised as the Black Knight, entered the tournaments at Ashby and won great glory. Then he wandered through his kingdom, meeting up with the Hermit of Copmanhurst (Friar Tuck) and Robin of Locksley (Robin Hood). Locksley in fact saved the King from an attempt on his life and together they besieged Torquilstone Castle, where Richard's enemies De Bracy and Front de Boeuf were holding out, with Rowena still their prisoner. Thanks to the King's victory at the Castle, Rowena and Ivanhoe were reunited, while Rebecca, hiding her love for Ivanhoe, left England with her father.

His origin

Ivanhoe was created by a great Scottish writer, Sir Walter Scott. His story *Ivanhoe* was published in 1819 and has been popular ever since. It has been translated into many different languages and turned into plays and films. Two popular British television series have been made of the Ivanhoe story, the first starring Roger Moore (more famous perhaps as The Saint on TV and James Bond in

the cinema), and the most recent starring Anthony Andrews.

James Bond

James Bond, secret agent 007, is the son of a Scottish father and a Swiss mother. He is one of the top agents in the British secret service which gives him a special licence – a licence to kill. As well as being a first-class shot, Bond is also a marvellous athlete and an expert at judo and karate. His brain is very quick too – he's even had to defuse an atom bomb only a matter of seconds before it was due to explode! He can fly anything from a spacecraft to an umbrella and he has the ability to understand the workings of the world's most brilliant criminal minds in order to defeat their evil plans.

Luckily for us, James Bond's on our side. He's a patriotic Briton through and through, and time and again he risks his own life to prevent some wicked Russian or criminal plot from harming Britain, or, worse still, from dominating the world.

Bond's principal adversaries belong to huge criminal organisations like SMERSH and SPECTRE, but the one who ranks as his greatest individual enemy is the evil agent, Blofeld – the man who is always seen stroking a white cat, and one who murdered Bond's wife, Tracy, on their wedding day.

In most of his adventures James Bond is called in by his boss, 'M', who tells him of the latest threat to world peace and gives him instructions to break whichever organisation is behind the plot and to kill its leader. His assignments take him to all parts of the world – and even into space.

In most cases Bond manages to penetrate the enemy organisation, but once inside it, he tends to get caught and face certain death – that is until a beautiful woman (who often works for the baddies until she meets James Bond) comes to release him and help him complete his mission!

His origin

James Bond was created by the British writer, Ian Fleming, who had worked for the secret service in real life. The first James Bond story, *Casino Royale*, was published in 1953, since when thirteen others have appeared and have never been out of print. The James Bond films have been just as successful, first with Sean Connery as 007 and more recently with Roger Moore as the hero.

King Arthur

Arthur, the great King of the Britons, was the son of Uther Pendragon, King of All England. But Arthur spent the early part of his life not knowing his true identity. Merlin, the mighty magician, had carefully planned Arthur's upbringing. He wanted the future king to be brought up as an ordinary boy, before he revealed himself as king by performing a great deed. So Arthur spent his boyhood in the home of Sir Ector, living side-by-side with Sir Ector's own son, Sir Kay, without any idea of who he really was.

Arthur's true destiny was revealed on New Year's Day, several years after King Uther's death. Sir Kay had entered a great tournament in London and Sir Ector had taken the two young men to London at Christmas. The city was buzzing with the news of a strange stone which had mysteriously appeared in a churchyard a few days before. On top of the stone was an anvil and sticking from the anvil was a sword. And around the stone was written: 'Whosoever pulls out this sword from this stone and anvil is the trueborn king of all England.'

Naturally every knight in London for the tournament had tried his strength at pulling the sword from the stone, but none of them had been able to budge it. So the day of the tournament came round with the sword still stuck fast in the stone, and the attention of the knights switched from that to the jousting field where they would be competing with the best in the land.

Sir Kay, Sir Ector and Arthur set out for the tournament and were well on their way before Sir Kay realised he had left his sword behind. He could hardly enter the tournament without it and Arthur rode back to fetch it for him. When he got back to the house where they were staying he found that everyone had gone to the tournament and the house was locked up. He knew he had to get Sir Kay a sword from somewhere and suddenly he remembered the sword in the stone which everyone had been talking about.

Arthur found the churchyard where the stone was standing, and, without bothering to read the inscription, took hold of the sword and pulled it easily from the stone. The truth of what had happened didn't dawn on him until he got back to the others, but then the word started to get about that an unknown youth had pulled the sword from the stone. At first the idea that Arthur was destined to be king was met with total disbelief, but the meaning of the words on the stone was unmistakeable, and since most of the knights present had failed to pull the sword from the stone, they had to admit that Arthur must indeed be the intended king. He was crowned king at Whitsuntide and he promised to rule his kingdom with justice throughout his life. Which is exactly what he did.

Soon after his coronation Arthur was riding with Merlin beside a lake when they suddenly saw a magnificent sword rising from the surface of the water. The sword was held aloft by an arm and while they were staring at it, a maiden walked across the water to Arthur and told him that the sword was named Excalibur and that he could have it. Before he rowed out to fetch it, Arthur had

to promise the maiden that he would return Excalibur when he died.

Armed with this magic sword Arthur gradually brought order to his troubled kingdom. In time he married Guinevere, the beautiful daughter of the King of Cameliard, and after their marriage Arthur established the famous Round Table around which he gathered one hundred faithful knights to serve him – and the most valiant and courageous of them all was Sir Lancelot.

Tragically it was Sir Lancelot, the greatest of the knights, who was to bring about its downfall. Ever since Lancelot had laid eyes on Queen Guinevere, he had loved her and she had loved him. They both loved Arthur too, but their love for each other was even greater and it was their secret love which broke the Round Table.

Two of Arthur's nephews, Sir Mordred and Sir Agravaine, plotted to ruin the queen and Lancelot, and even when one of their plots to expose Lancelot and Guinevere failed, Sir Mordred escaped and continued his feud against them. Meanwhile a civil war had broken out between Arthur and Lancelot in which many knights were killed. And when Arthur attempted to make peace, his supporters demanded that Lancelot should be banished. An even more serious threat came when Sir Mordred entered the war in the hope of killing Arthur, taking his crown and making Guinevere his own queen.

The final battle of the war was fought somewhere in Cornwall, and all but a few knights were killed. Eventually Arthur and Mordred came face to face. They fought a long duel which Arthur at last won when he gave Mordred a mortal blow. But as he was dying, Arthur's wicked nephew stabbed his uncle and Arthur knew that the blow would kill him too. He asked two of his knights who had survived the battle, Sir Bedivere and Sir Lucan, to carry him to the sea shore. There Sir Bedivere threw Excalibur far out into the water, where an arm reached above the waves and caught it. Then a mysterious boat appeared and carried Arthur away to Avalon, where his wound was to be healed and from where, so the legend tells, he will return one day, when his country needs him. And somewhere lies his grave on which are written the words: 'Here lies Arthur, the once and future king.'

His origin

The King Arthur of the story is really a character created by medieval storytellers, who used much older British legends about a hero king. No one knows for certain if King Arthur ever existed, but if he did, he probably lived in western England, or in Wales, during the fifth century AD, when he led the British against the Saxons, who were invading from the East. Since the Romans hadn't left Britain long before King Arthur is supposed to have lived, some people believe that Arthur was probably more like a Roman general than a medieval knight in armour.

The Lone Ranger

The Lone Ranger was the so-called Robin Hood of the Wild West. The sole survivor of a group of Texas Rangers who had been gunned down by a gang of cowardly outlaws in an ambush, he vowed to devote the rest of his life to avenging his fallen comrades, and from that moment he put on his famous black eye-mask and began his personal crusade against murder and robbery in the West.

His only real allies were his faithful white horse, Silver, and Tonto, the Indian friend whom he'd rescued from the villainous Cavendish gang. Apart from them the Lone Ranger lived up to his name: he was a loner and no one ever discovered his true identity.

In spite of the fame of his successes, which quickly spread throughout the frontier territory, it wasn't unusual for people to receive his help without ever realising who it was who'd come to their aid. Usually it wasn't until the Lone Ranger and Tonto were riding off into the distance, with the hero shouting his famous victory cry 'Hi-Yo, Silver!' that it dawned on them who the man in the eye-mask was. And usually the only clue he left behind to show that he'd been in a place, was a silver bullet.

His origin

The Lone Ranger started life in a story written for American radio by Fran Striker in the 1930s. This became so popular that it was quickly followed by a cartoon strip. Then came feature films and finally a television series starring Clayton Moore, with Jay Silverheels as Tonto.

Nancy Drew

If you're going to be a detective, there's no doubt that you get a head start if your Dad happens to be a lawyer – and that's just what Nancy, daughter of Carson Drew, has found. Nancy's taken an interest in her father's work since she was very young and now she's a little older she often gives him a helping hand. Her father reckons that she's got 'a natural talent for digging into interesting cases', which is helpful for him since many of the enemies he's made through his work frequently crop up to menace him – until Nancy sends them packing.

Most of her adventures seem to take place in old, spooky houses, in secret, underground passages and in eerie damp caves, but Nancy is always brave enough and clever enough to deal with the most frightening and difficult situations.

To help her in her investigations Nancy has three companions – George, a boyish-looking girl, with short, brown hair, who's just as brave as Nancy herself; Bess, who's plumper and prettier than George, but gets scared more easily; and Nancy's boyfriend, Ned, who goes to college out of

town, but who always turns up to help solve a mystery when he's needed.

Her origin

If you look at the front of any Nancy Drew story, you'll see that the author's name is given as Carolyn Keene. In fact this was the pen-name used by Edward L. Stratemeyer, the man who also created the Hardy Boys. Stratemeyer founded a syndicate for writing his stories and many people were involved in writing the Nancy Drew adventures. The first time Nancy Drew appeared was in 1930 in the *Secret of the Old Clock*. She's been solving cases for over fifty years now both in books, films and on television, where Pamela Sue Martin plays the teenage detective.

Paddington Bear

Paddington Bear is a honey-bear from darkest Peru with a passion for marmalade sandwiches. He lived with his aunt Lucy in Peru until she decided to go and live in a home for retired bears and advised her nephew to stow away on a boat bound for England. Aunt Lucy was a wise old bear and Paddington followed her advice. He found a boat sailing to England and slipped on board.

When he arrived in England Paddington made his way to London by train and reached Paddington Station where Mr and Mrs Brown and their daughter Judy came across him quite by chance and decided to take him home with them. Since he didn't seem to have a name they called him Paddington, after the station where they'd found him.

Paddington's a well-meaning bear with a warm heart, but he is dreadfully clumsy. He's pretty scruffy-looking too, and you will usually see him wearing a shabby old hat (once his uncle's proud possession) and either a duffle coat, or a yellow mac.

Of course, Paddington's great advantage over other bears is that he can communicate with humans and living with the Brown's he's treated just like any other member of the family. He likes going to the theatre; he likes painting; and he feels as at home in London as he did in the Peruvian jungles. He's a remarkable bear by any standards, but of all the superheroes in the book he's certainly the most accident-prone.

His origin

Paddington Bear was created by writer Michael Bond and the first story *A Bear Called Paddington*, appeared in 1958.

Peter Pan

Peter Pan was the little boy who never grew up. He was born in London and when he was still only a week old, he flew out of his bedroom one night and met up with the fairies in the Kensington Gardens, who welcomed him as a Betwixt-and-Between. Sometimes Peter went to look at his old home and peep through the bedroom window at his own little bed, but one night he arrived and found the window barred, with a new baby asleep in the bed. From then on he knew there could be no going back.

Peter went off to live in the Never-Never Land and took with him a gang of companions called the Lost Boys, young children who had got lost when they fell out of their prams. Peter used to fly to London regularly and one night visited the house of Mr and Mrs Darling and their three children, Wendy, John and Michael. Mr and Mrs Darling were out, so when Peter had taught the three children to fly he took them off to Never-Never Land, where they had plenty of adventures, involving a band of Red Indians, and a crew of rascally pirates led by the wicked Captain Hook. Eventually the Darling children persuaded Peter to take them home again, and Mr and Mrs Darling asked Peter to stay and live with them in London. Peter wasn't having any of it. He knew that if he stayed with the Darlings he would have to become a real boy and the one thing Peter Pan was certain of was: he *never* wanted to grow up.

His origin
Peter Pan was created by a Scottish playwright, Sir James Barrie. In 1902 he wrote *The Little White*

Bird, which later became *Peter Pan in Kensington Gardens* and two years later he wrote what many people think is his best play, *Peter Pan*. As well as inventing the character of Peter Pan, James Barrie also invented the name Wendy.

Popeye

Popeye's story started in America one day back in 1929 when Olive Oyl, her brother Castor, and her boyfriend Ham Gravy, were planning a trip to Dice Island. They had a big yacht for the trip but needed a sailor to man her. Walking along the docks, Castor saw an odd-looking character. 'Hey there, are you a sailor?' 'Ja think I'm a cowboy?' drawled Popeye. 'Okay,' said Castor, 'You're hired.'

At first Popeye seemed to be something of a coward, but when Castor chased him up the mast of the ship, Popeye let fly with the first of his famous punches, and Castor was sent rolling down the deck.

As a rule, Popeye's punches are reserved for his arch-enemy, Bluto, his chief rival for the love of the skinny Olive Oyl. Bluto is a blackbearded and black-hearted bully, a huge monster of a man.

Apart from Bluto, Olive and the rest of the Oyl family, other Popeye favourites include Poop Deck Pappy, Popeye's father, his nephews Peepeye and

Poopeye, Mr Geezil, the Sea Hag and a confidence trickster called J. Wellington Wimpey, famous for saying 'I'll gladly pay you Tuesday for a hamburger today.'

Popeye, of course, is renowned for his trick of squeezing spinach out of a can. Fortified with spinach he will happily drill a hole through steel with his big toe or tackle a gorilla with his little finger. His fighting spirit knows no bounds.

His origin

Popeye was created by Elzie Crisler Segar – known throughout his life simply as E. C. Segar because he refused to tell anyone his first name. Popeye first appeared in the cinema in *The Thimble Theater* in February 1929, but he became so popular that the title was changed to *Popeye* three years later. Popeye has appeared in over two hundred cartoons and in 1980 a full length feature film of Popeye was released with Robin Williams starring as the spinach-eating sailor, and Shelley Duvall playing the part of Olive Oyl.

Robin Hood

Robin Hood lived in the twelfth century at the time of King Richard I. For most of his reign King Richard was away from England fighting the Crusades in the Holy Land, and in his absence the country was ruled by his younger brother, Prince

John. John was closely allied with other powerful Normans, who were determined to stamp out what was left of the old Saxon power in England, so that they could have complete control over the kingdom.

Robin Hood and the men that gathered round him were outlaws who waged a private war against the Normans in and around the great Sherwood Forest, robbing from the rich and giving what they stole to the poor and needy, who were usually Saxons. Most of Robin's men had been made outlaws for minor crimes, such as killing one of the king's deer to feed their own starving families. Before becoming an outlaw himself Robin had been a knight, Sir Robin of Locksley.

Under Prince John the ordinary people of England had to pay very high taxes and when it was announced that King Richard had been captured while he was on his way home from the Holy Land, the taxes became even heavier to pay for his release. Prince John was in Nottingham when his brother's capture was announced and, plotting with his chief conspirator, Sir Guy of Gisbourne, he planned to seize the throne for himself. But Robin Hood had plans of his own and he and his men declared war on the Prince and Sir Guy.

The outlaws' first act was a brilliant ambush of the Normans as they made their way back to London with the taxes that had been collected in and around Nottingham. The Norman soldiers were completely overwhelmed by Robin's men, and the High Sheriff of Nottingham, Sir Guy of Gisbourne, and many others, were taken prisoner. Among them was a royal ward, Lady Marian, who had originally been horrified by Robin Hood's attacks on the Normans, but when she heard what Robin was trying to do for the people, her opinion changed and she became one of the outlaw's loyal supporters.

Once Robin had released all his prisoners, Sir Guy, the High Sheriff and Prince John plotted to put an end to the outlaw and they devised a scheme to capture him. It was known far and wide that Robin Hood was the best archer in England and the High Sheriff decided that if an archery contest were held and if Robin could be persuaded to compete in it, he would be sure to win and the Normans would be sure of catching him. What the Sheriff needed was a bait to catch Robin, so he announced that Lady Marian would personally present the prize to the winning archer.

The plot worked like a dream. Robin Hood couldn't resist entering the competition, although he went in disguise, and as expected, he won it. But instead of being awarded first prize he was seized by the Normans and flung into prison. He would certainly have lost his life it hadn't been for Lady Marian who warned his men and arranged for them to rescue their leader. Lady Marian paid dearly for this, though, and was thrown into prison and sentenced to death in Robin's place.

Meanwhile King Richard had been released and had returned to his kingdom with a party of knights, all of them disguised as monks. He had heard about his brother's plans to become king and so joined forces with Robin Hood to defeat Prince John once and for all.

At the very moment when the wicked Prince was about to be crowned, one of the large group of 'monks' attending the coronation, threw back his cowl and declared that he was the rightful King of England. Sir Guy yelled that this was just a trick and ordered the soldiers to capture the monks, but King Richard's men and the outlaws had hidden weapons under their cassocks and a furious fight broke out. Naturally, Prince John and his men were defeated and, thanks to Robin Hood, good King Richard was able to take control of his kingdom once again.

His origin

Robin Hood has been a popular English hero for hundreds of years, but nobody knows if he ever really existed. There have been stories, plays, films and even a Walt Disney cartoon film about him, and he must be one of the longest-living of all the superheroes.

Robinson Crusoe

The adventures of one of the most famous sailors ever to be shipwrecked started when Robinson

Crusoe, a young English sailor, was washed ashore on a desert island. Apart from the ship's dog and the two ship's cats, he found that he was the only survivor and to add to his feelings of loneliness he also found that there were no other people living on the island.

Fortunately the wrecked ship didn't sink immediately and before she went down Crusoe was able to salvage many useful weapons, tools and provisions, all of which helped to keep him going for the next twenty-eight years!

At first Crusoe lived on the island in a cave. Around this he built a fence of strong stakes to keep out wild animals and inside his 'fortress' he stored all his food and equipment.

In the early months he was desperately lonely and afraid. He became ill; he survived a hurricane; he even lived through an earthquake that rocked the island. But after ten months of living alone he plucked up courage to make his first attempts to explore the island and found to his delight that it had a rich supply of fruit as well as fresh water. So he built himself a rough shelter in a green valley to give himself a 'country house' as well as one by the sea.

On his first real expedition Crusoe crossed the island and was thrilled to see land in the distance. When he got back to his camp he tried to make a canoe, but once he had built it he found it was so heavy he couldn't move it and when he next tried to make a boat he made it much smaller!

As the years went by Crusoe settled into his life on the island. He bred goats and used their skins to make his clothes. He crew simple crops and made further explorations of the island. It was while he was on one of these that he came across a terrifying sight – a human footprint in the sand!

A little later he came across an even more frightening discovery: a stretch of beach littered with human bones – the remains of cannibal feasts. Crusoe realised his danger and immediately searched for a safer place to live, settling for a huge cave on a hill, which gave him a good look-out position. It was from here that he saw his first human beings for many years, when he watched a party of cannibals come ashore and feast on their victims.

It was at another cannibal feast that Crusoe found himself a companion, a young native who was about to be eaten by his captors. Crusoe saved this man and named him Friday, after the day of the week on which they had met. From then on Crusoe's life changed.

At first he was very cautious about Friday, fearing that Friday might try to kill him. But after some time the two men grew accustomed to each other, and Crusoe started teaching Friday to speak English and taught him about Christianity.

When more cannibals landed on their island Crusoe and Friday drove them off and in so doing rescued two more prisoners, a Spanish sailor and Friday's father. And escape from the island finally came to Crusoe and Friday when they rescued another group of prisoners who turned out to be English sailors who had been put ashore by the rest of their crew, which had mutinied. Crusoe helped the ship's captain put down the mutiny and in return he was given a free passage home to England where he landed thirty-three years after he had set sail.

His origin

The story of Robinson Crusoe was written by a famous sixteenth-century English writer, Daniel Defoe. He based the story on the adventures of a real sailor, Alexander Selkirk, who had spent many years living alone on a desert island before being rescued.

The Saint

Simon Templar's initials are S.T. St is the abbreviation of Saint; and that's why Simon Templar calls himself The Saint. Tall, muscular and athletic, The Saint is a skilled sportsman and a crack shot. He's a man who enjoys the best things in life. He likes good food, clothes from the best tailors, fast cars and beautiful women. The Saint is a man of the world and he travels the world too, visiting exciting, glamorous places and meeting people from every walk of life.

When it comes to fighting crime, The Saint

usually tries to stick on the right side of the law, but he has his own ways of doing things, and these frequently end up with him getting into trouble with the police. There's poor Inspector Teal of Scotland Yard, who looks on Simon Templar as anything but a saint because of the number of times that he's found the sleuth meddling in one of his cases. The Inspector's main problem is that he never gets much closer to The Saint than finding one of his calling cards – with its distinctive stick figure topped with a halo.

Simon Templar devotes his considerable energies to catching crooks and bringing them to heel, even if it means stepping outside the law at times – as it did when he was hired by a group of powerful New York citizens to kill six of the city's top gangsters. He bumped off the criminals and then made it hot-foot to South America, one step ahead of the FBI, to join in a revolution!

His origin

The Saint has a lot in common with the man who brought him into being, Leslie Charteris. Like Simon Templar, Charteris was an adventurer who'd worked all over the world in most jobs from tin-mining to professional card playing. Charteris wrote his first Saint novel in 1928. In the last fifty years over forty Saint novels and more than a hundred Saint stories have appeared. Today The Saint is probably best known as the handsome television hero played first by Roger Moore, and, more recently, by Ian Ogilvy.

The Scarlet Pimpernel

If you know something about natural history, you may know that the Scarlet Pimpernel is a small flower that only appears for a very short time. Even if you didn't know it, Sir Percy Blakeney, an eighteenth-century English gentleman, certainly did, because he chose this as his undercover name for highly dangerous work in France after the French Revolution.

Sir Percy was an English aristocrat, who, like many of the English aristocracy, was horrified at the widespread execution of French aristocrats that was taking place in the so-called 'Reign of Terror', which followed the overthrow of the French monarchy. Sir Percy did more than show his dismay at what was happening; he risked his life in travelling to France in various disguises in order to rescue French aristocrats who faced execution.

To most people Sir Percy appeared to be a bored, rude, lazy good-for-nothing, and this was the image he tried hard to create, since it acted as a perfect cover for his real work in travelling secretly to and fro from France where he would join the huge crowds that gathered whenever there was to be an execution. Sometimes Sir Percy would be disguised as an old woman, sometimes as a country bumpkin. No one would know he was there until the blade of the guillotine was about to fall, when Sir Percy would spring into action, rescue the victims and rush them to the coast and safety across the sea to England.

No one ever knew the identity of the Scarlet Pimpernel, but it wasn't long before everyone knew of his daring exploits. The revolutionary government in France started to get very embarrassed by the number of aristocrats that were being rescued and they sent one of their best agents to England to find out who the Pimpernel really was.

Chauvelin, the agent, didn't have any luck at first and his superiors told him that he'd lose his own head if he didn't expose the Scarlet Pimpernel before he returned to France. Without suspecting Sir Percy at all, Chauvelin contacted his wife, Lady Blakeney, who was a French aristocrat herself, and whose brother was still being held in France. Chauvelin made a bargain with her, offering to free her brother if she would help him catch the Scarlet Pimpernel. If she refused to help him, Chauvelin told her, her brother would die.

Of course Lady Blakeney had no idea that her husband was the Scarlet Pimpernel and un- wittingly she agreed to help the scheming Frenchman. But, when the Scarlet Pimpernel was finally caught in Calais, she was horrified to find that the dashing hero was none other than her apparently meek husband.

It was now time for Sir Percy to strike a bargain with Chauvelin. If Lady Blakeney was released and allowed to travel safely back to England, Sir Percy agreed to go straight in front of a firing-squad. Chauvelin was overjoyed at this and Sir Percy went out to face his death. Chauvelin heard the gunfire and thought that all his problems were over, until Sir Percy reappeared a few minutes later, alive and well. The men in the firing-squad had all been in his service – and the Scarlet Pimpernel lived to continue his daring rescue missions.

His origin

The Scarlet Pimpernel was created by a Hungarian writer, Baroness Orczy, in 1905. She did not know a word of English until she was fifteen and yet wrote all her books in English.

Sherlock Holmes

Sherlock Holmes, the world's most famous detective, was born in the North Riding of Yorkshire in a farmstead called Mycroft. He solved his first case when he was a twenty-one-year-old student at Oxford University and then began his long and extraordinary career as a private detective without equal.

At the beginning of 1881 Holmes moved into new rooms in London at 221B Baker Street. Looking for someone to share the rooms with him he met an ex-army doctor named Henry Watson.

From this chance meeting, Holmes and Watson developed a life-long friendship. In fact if it hadn't been for Dr Watson we wouldn't have any record of the life and work of Sherlock Holmes, as it was Watson who recorded all his cases for posterity, although Holmes himself did not always approve of what Watson wrote.

Sherlock Holmes was very tall and thin, with a sharp, hooked nose. He smoked foul-smelling tobacco, played the violin like a master violinist and conducted complicated scientific experiments in his rooms. He had a brilliant mind and a wide knowledge of science, law and medicine, but his greatest skill lay in his ability to take in the tiniest details of what he saw. Holmes would be able to seize on clues that professional detectives either ignored, or didn't see in the first place. And coupled with this he had the sort of quick-thinking mind that could put together facts which didn't seem to have any connection, and, by using them, work out exactly what had happened in each case and 'whodunnit'.

Dr Watson was nothing like as intelligent or as quickwitted as Holmes, but he was sensible and dependable, which was just what Holmes needed in a companion. Among the other characters in Sherlock Holmes's life were his brother Mycroft, who was even more brilliant than the detective; Mrs Hudson, his kindly landlady in Baker Street; Billy, the page-boy at 221B; and Inspector Lestrade, the detective from Scotland Yard, who

often worked side-by-side with Holmes on his cases.

As for his enemies, Holmes's greatest criminal adversary was the evil Professor Moriarty, with whom he finally struggled violently over a high waterfall, before they both fell into the foaming water beneath. Sherlock Holmes was presumed to have drowned, but in fact he returned to carry on his remarkable career.

Holmes was a genius, but there was one occasion when he was outwitted himself – by a woman. She was a beautiful and brilliant opera singer, Irene Adler. She was the only woman that Holmes ever loved and when she died, Holmes retired to Sussex to keep bees and Mrs Hudson left Baker Street to act as his housekeeper.

His origin

Sherlock Holmes was created by a young Scottish doctor, Arthur Conan Doyle. The first story in which he appeared was *A Study in Scarlet*, which was published at Christmas 1887. Since then Conan Doyle's many Sherlock Holmes stories have been read all over the world and there have been dozens of films, plays and television programmes about the famous detective, with his distinctive deerstalker hat, pipe and magnifying glass.

Spiderman

In real life Spiderman was an American high school student called Peter Parker. Peter was different from his classmates, about as different as you'd expect anyone to be who'd been bitten by a radioactive spider! When Peter recovered from the bite he found that several things about him had changed. For one thing he found that he'd suddenly acquired superhuman powers of strength and endurance and, for another, he discovered that he was now a human spider, who could swing across town on gigantic spiders' webs to tackle criminals like The Vulture.

Spiderman's different from other superheroes, who tend to leave their human senses and weaknesses behind them when they slip into their superhero costumes and go roaring off to do battle. Spiderman, on the other hand, is both human and superhuman at the same time. He once took off after an opponent in a snowstorm saying to himself: '. . . if this cold spell doesn't break up soon, I'm liable to be the only web-crawler in town wearing a muffler . . . and mittens! These long-underwear rags are great for the super-hero image . . . but a fella can freeze to death in weather like this!'

In spite of his human failings, Spiderman relentlessly pursues his foes, overcoming all of their fiendish powers and bringing justice to his city – and, in a way, his action requires even

73

greater courage and determination than that of many other superheroes, who aren't affected by worries and doubts like his. Spiderman's got a superhero's body and mind, but the spirit and sensitivity of an ordinary high-school student.

Just to add to his difficulties, Spiderman also has to look after his Aunt May, an old lady who has had several heart attacks. What's more, Spiderman is also hounded by the police from time to time, and by newspaper publisher, J. Jonah Jameson, who hates him. And to cap it all, one of Spiderman's best friends turns out to be the child of his deadliest enemy, the Green Goblin. Being a superhero has brought Spiderman his fair share of glory, but it's brought him a bucketful of problems too!

His origin

Spiderman was one of the new generation of superheroes created in the 1960s. The editor of *Marvel Comics*, Stan Lee, and artist, Steve Ditko, started his adventures in August 1962, and since then he's become one of the most popular superheroes, featuring in a very successful television series as well as comics.

Superman

'Just before the doomed planet, Krypton, exploded to fragments, a scientist placed his infant son within an experimental rocket-ship, launching it toward earth!' – that's how the most famous superhero of them all made his escape from the home of his forefathers and found his way to earth, because the baby that escaped from Krypton grew up to be none other than Superman.

The rocket-ship crashed to earth in the United States and when the baby had climbed out of the wreckage it was found and placed in the local orphanage – where everyone was more than a little alarmed by a tiny tot that could lift heavy furniture with a single hand and more than relieved when a Mr and Mrs Kent arrived and said they would like to adopt the baby boy.

The Kents called their new son Clark. They brought him up like a normal boy, at least they did their best bearing in mind that he could jump over skyscrapers, pick up an entire car, run as fast as an express train, and had a skin that was as tough as armour plating. Clark loved his adopted parents and listened to what they had told him about his amazing powers. They believed that when the time came, he must use his superhuman strength to help humanity. And when they died, Clark knew that the time had come to turn himself into Superman: 'the champion of the oppressed, the physical marvel who had sworn to devote his existence to helping those in need!'

As a cover for this role, Clark took on the identity of a newspaper reporter, a timid, shy man with glasses, who wasn't especially good at his job and seemed a bit of a weakling. In fact Clark Kent, the reporter, became the exact opposite of the hero who flew through the skies chasing criminals and saving people from earthquakes, floods and other natural disasters.

Being a newspaper reporter did have its advantages. Clark Kent knew when trouble was about to strike sooner than anyone else. All he had to do then was to disappear into a lift or a telephone box to transform himself into Superman, the red-caped hero with the skin-tight blue costume and the large red 'S' emblazoned on his chest.

As time passed his powers increased. Once he had learned to fly, he developed several types of X-ray vision, as well as an invulnerability against almost anything that could be fired against him. There was only one substance that was deadly to Superman, a substance which would certainly kill him if he touched it even lightly: green Kryptonite, lumps of his own planet that had been blown far and wide into space when Krypton exploded.

Kryptonite was not the only worry in Superman's life. Much nearer home was Lois Lane, who worked in the same newspaper office. Superman had saved Lois's life once and she'd been madly in love with him ever since. But while Lois loved Superman, she had nothing but scorn for Clark Kent who was deeply in love with her. This put Superman into a fix and he had to settle for accepting Lois's love as Superman, while suffering her contempt as Clark Kent. There wasn't anything he could do about it. And, of course, the last thing he wanted was for Lois, or anyone else, to discover that the weedy Clark Kent was really Superman.

His origin

Superman was the brain-child of two seventeen-year-old American boys, Jerry Siegal and Joe Shuster. Jerry wrote the captions and Joe drew the pictures. For five years they worked at perfecting their superhero before a comic book publisher agreed to accept their work. The publisher paid 130 dollars for it. It was the best deal he ever made. Superman has been selling like hot cakes ever since. He is featured in cartoons, on stage, on television and in films, the most recent of which were the three box-office hits starring Christopher Reeve.

Supergirl

As you might expect, Supergirl is related to Superman, in fact they are cousins. Supergirl is actually the last survivor of Argo City, which was part of the planet Krypton before it was ripped apart by the explosion which destroyed it. In the destruction of the planet, Argo City was hurled clear into space, still in one piece. But the ground on which it stood was soon transformed into the deadly substance Kryptonite. The inhabitants of Argo City covered every inch of the ground with lead-sheeting to prevent the Kryptonite from escaping, but this protection couldn't last for ever and before long the lead was punctured by a meteorite shower and the lethal Kryptonite rays started to leak.

When Superman's uncle, Zor-el realised the terrible fate that awaited his city, he sent his teenage daughter, Kal-el, to join her cousin on earth. When she arrived, Kal-el took on the identity of an ordinary girl called Linda Lee, and she wore a brown wig to cover her dazzling blonde hair.

To begin with she lived in Midvale Orphanage, but although many people offered to adopt the beautiful girl, she didn't leave the orphanage until two years after her arrival on earth, because Superman had been carefully training his cousin in secret and didn't want his work interrupted. However, when the time was right, Supergirl went to live with Mr and Mrs Danvers, and changed her name to Linda Lee Danvers. A year later Superman told her that her long period of training was over and that it was time for her to join him in his war against crime. But, like Superman himself, Supergirl maintained her ordinary identity in daily life.

Her origin

Supergirl appeared much later than Superman. It wasn't until May 1959 that she joined her cousin as a character created by writer Mort Weisinger, and artist, Otto Binder.

Tarzan

Tarzan the Lord of the Jungle was a real lord in his own right – an English lord. When he was still a little boy, Tarzan and his parents set out on a daring journey into the jungles of Africa, but disaster struck and Tarzan's parents died in the jungle. The little boy was saved by friendly apes and they brought up the little human as though he were one of their own offspring.

With the apes Tarzan learned to live as a jungle animal. He learned to move through the trees and through the jungle paths with the stealth of a wild beast. And, most important, he learned to communicate with all the animals, who didn't look on him as a hostile human, but as one of their own.

But Tarzan couldn't forget his human background and while he was learning all he could of jungle craft and animal lore, he also taught himself to read and write, so that by the time he was a fully grown man, Tarzan could live at ease in the jungle, yet was still able to communicate and live with human beings. In fact when he was a young man Tarzan left the jungle and travelled widely throughout the rest of the world. When he returned to the jungle he fell in love with an

American girl, Jane Porter, who was also an explorer.

Of course, the Tarzan that most of us know today is a little different from the original. He is still the Lord of the Jungle, the man who is able to summon the animals with his famous call, the one who can swing through trees like an ape and fight alligators with his bare hands, but he doesn't look very much like a lost English aristocrat who has travelled the world!

Over the years Tarzan has had many jungle adventures but perhaps the most famous is the one when he and Jane became involved with a party of English explorers searching for the fabled elephants' graveyard. The elephants were Tarzan's friends and he wasn't prepared to lead the explorers to their sacred resting place so that they could steal the valuable ivory from the dead elephants. The explorers were determined, greedy men, who knew that a huge fortune awaited them if they could only find their way to the site where all the elephant carcasses lay. So they decided to wound an elephant in the hope that it would lead them to the graveyard, where it would die alongside its ancestors. At the same time the explorers shot Tarzan, left him for dead, and made off with Jane.

The jungle animals found the wounded Tarzan and nursed him back to life so that he could go after the explorers and prevent them from carrying out their wicked plan. As it happened, others beat him to it. Travelling through the most dangerous part of the jungle, the explorers aroused a hostile tribe and while they were preparing to carry the ivory away from the elephants' graveyard, the tribesmen attacked and killed the Englishmen. They'd probably have killed Jane too if Tarzan and his elephants hadn't arrived in the nick of time to save her.

His origin

The original Tarzan was created by an American writer, Edgar Rice Burroughs, who never set foot in Africa. This didn't prevent him writing numerous stories about Tarzan's African adventures. He sold over twenty-five million copies of his Tarzan books, which eventually led to film and television companies putting Tarzan on the screen. At one time an American Olympic swimming champion, Johnny Weissmuller, played Tarzan, and many people still think that he was the best Lord of the Jungle, even though most of his films were made over forty years ago. The most recent cinema version of Tarzan was made in 1981. It starred a very revealing Bo Derek as Jane and this time the film was judged as unsuitable viewing for children and given an X rating.

The Three Musketeers

The first half of the seventeenth century was a very restless time in France. The king, Louis XIII, was weak and the country was virtually governed by the powerful Cardinal Richelieu. There was bitter fighting between the Catholics and the Protestants (called Huguenots) and what amounted to private armies roamed the country picking fights with each other.

At the same time it was an exciting period in which to live and one in which young men with ambition could fight their way to positions of great importance. And in the case of one young nobleman, 'D'Artagnan, the position he wanted was that of a Musketeer, one of the trusted servants of the Queen of France herself.

D'Artagnan left his home for Paris, where he had an introduction to the commander of the Musketeers. But while he was in the city he met three musketeers and got involved in a duel with each of them in turn. The Musketeers were named Porthos, Athos and Aramis and together they joined in a pact of eternal friendship with D'Artagnan.

The Musketeers were regularly involved in fights with the men employed by Cardinal Richelieu and it wasn't long before D'Artagnan became caught up in this feud. The Cardinal himself was plotting to win greater personal power by discrediting the Queen, whom he knew had given a set of twelve diamonds to an English visitor, the Duke of Buckingham, after she had received them as a present from her husband, the King.

Richelieu arranged for a ball to be held at which he knew the Queen would be expected to wear the diamonds, and then before she had time to send to the Duke of Buckingham to have them returned, he sent one of his agents to England to steal two of the diamonds. The agent he chose was a beautiful but wicked woman, Milady, who had previously been married to D'Artagnan's new friend, Athos.

As soon as the Queen heard about the ball she sent D'Artagnan and the others to the Duke of Buckingham as well, to bring the diamonds back to Paris. On the way they were pursued by the Cardinal's men, and one by one Porthos, Athos and Aramis were left behind fighting, while D'Artagnan reached England alone. Luckily he managed to get to the Duke, who had two replicas made to replace the missing diamonds, and when D'Artagnan returned to Paris the Queen was able to wear them at the ball, foiling the Cardinal's evil plan.

D'Artagnan's troubles weren't over after this success. He and the others were sent to help defend the port of La Rochelle, which was under siege, and while there Milady attempted to murder him. Again her plot failed, so together with Cardinal Richelieu she planned to travel to England again, this time to warn the Duke of Buckingham against interfering in the siege of La Rochelle, on the side of the Cardinal's enemies, the Huguenots.

The Musketeers heard of Milady's plan and arranged for her to be captured and imprisoned in

England on landing. But the scheming woman was able to win over her English captor and even persuaded him to assassinate the Duke of Buckingham.

Back in France Milady committed her final crime by poisoning a serving woman of the Queen's, with whom D'Artagnan was in love. However, she was captured after this and was executed.

Milady's death put D'Artagnan in danger once more, and when he was called before Cardinal Richelieu his life was in the balance. The Cardinal, however, realising that a man like D'Artagnan was a useful servant to the crown and not a man to be wasted by an execution, appointed him to the rank of Lieutenant in the Musketeers.

Their origin

The story of *The Three Musketeers* was the work of a French writer, Alexandre Dumas, and it was first published in 1843, when it became an immediate best-seller. The story has been popular ever since. It's been filmed many times, most recently in 1973 when Michael York, Oliver Reed, Frank Finlay and Richard Chamberlain played the Musketeers, Charlton Heston was Cardinal Richelieu, and Faye Dunaway, Milady.

Tin Tin

Tin Tin is a round-faced teenage reporter, with a funny tuft of hair sticking up from the top of his head. Although he is a journalist, Tin Tin spends most of his time solving crimes and mysteries – and is a most accomplished detective.

Tin Tin's adventures have taken him from treasure islands to mountainous kingdoms in the Balkans. He's been to outer space and to the bottom of the sea. He can fly an aeroplane, shoot a gun like a marksman and put his brain to work to tackle the most difficult and complicated of cases – always with success!

During his adventures he's met with some valuable friends and exchanged blows with some noted villains. Thompson and Thompson, the twins who dress identically in bowler hats and dark suits, are detectives by profession, though they usually manage to get into such a muddle that it takes all Tin Tin's skill and patience to sort them out. Captain Haddock, the rum-drinking, tough-talking, black-bearded sailor is probably Tin Tin's closest ally, except for Snowy, Tin Tin's white-haired terrier. Captain Haddock is very well-meaning, but he does tend to get carried away, especially when he's had one too many swigs of rum!

His origin

Tin Tin's immense popularity for over fifty years is

thanks to his Belgian creator, the cartoonist, Hergé. The first Tin Tin story appeared in a Belgian newspaper in 1929 and since then over thirty stories have been translated into thirty languages. There have been television cartoons, two feature films and a play about Tin Tin.

William Tell

According to legend William Tell was a huntsman who lived in Uri in Switzerland, in the fourteenth century. He was famous for his skill with the crossbow and it was claimed that he could shoot an apple off a tree at a distance of a hundred paces.

For centuries Switzerland had been ruled by the powerful Hapsburg Empire and the bailiff in charge of William Tell's part of Switzerland was a man called Gessler.

One day Tell went with his young son Walter to the village at Altdorf. They were walking through the market place when Tell saw a cap that had been hung on a pole. He didn't take any notice of this and carried on walking until he was arrested by two soldiers, who told him that Gessler had ordered everyone in the village to bow down and salute his cap, as a token of his power.

As Tell was being questioned by the soldiers Gessler happened to ride by and when he heard that the famous huntsman had been arrested he

offered to free him on one condition – that he shot an apple from Walter's head at a distance of a hundred paces.

Reluctantly Tell agreed. He took two arrows, stuck one in his belt and placed the other on his crossbow. Then, taking a steady aim he fired at the apple and shot it straight through the centre. Everyone watching cried out in amazement, even Gessler, but before he released Tell, he asked him why he had drawn two arrows. Tell replied bravely that he'd been going to kill Gessler with the second arrow, if the first one had killed Walter.

This made Gessler furious and he immediately ordered Tell to be locked in prison for the rest of his life. The castle in which he was to be imprisoned lay on the far side of a lake and as the boat in which they were crossing reached the centre of the lake a huge storm hit them. Tell was the most experienced steersman on board and Gessler had him released to steer the boat to safety. But as they approached the shore, Tell jumped clear of the boat and escaped with his crossbow and arrows. Once he'd got away from his captors, he hid in the under-growth beside the path along which he knew Gessler would be riding, and when he came into sight, Tell fired an arrow straight through Gessler's heart.

This, you might say, was the first shot in Switzerland's struggle for independence. Once he had killed Gessler, Tell gathered all his country-men and began to attack the Hapsburg castles, slowly driving the hated rulers out of Switzerland until the whole country was free of them. And Switzerland has been an independent country ever since.

His origin

Plays, operas, films and television programmes have been written and made about William Tell, but most historians agree that he probably never existed which must make him the most famous Swiss who never lived.

Wonder Woman

Wonder Woman began life as an Amazonian princess. The Amazons were a powerful group of warriors in the world of Greek legends and what made them unusual was that all of them were women. They were led by a mighty queen, Hippolyte, and Wonder Woman was Queen Hippolyte's daughter.

Wonder Woman was brought up on Paradise Island, where time stood still and all men were forbidden. There she and her sisters lived contentedly for hundreds of years until 1941, when the United States entered the Second World War and Wonder Woman abandoned the security of Paradise Island to throw her weight behind the American war effort. Dressed in a patriotic costume of red, white, blue and yellow – very like a female Captain America in fact – Wonder Woman took on the toughest opponents including Mars, the God of War! It didn't matter who she came up against – Wonder Woman was sure to lay them out cold. She wasn't totally invincible, she had one tiny flaw. If her bracelets of submission were chained together by a man, Wonder Woman would lose all her superhuman strength.

Naturally Wonder Woman was equipped with amazing gadgets to help her save the world from evil and destruction, among the most useful of which were her golden lasso and her invisible robot plane. As an Amazon, of course, she can also summon her warrior sisters to come to her aid. And though she is supposed to hate men, there is one man whom Wonder Woman can't help loving very much: he's a handsome air force pilot, Steve Trevor.

Like so many superheroes and heroines, Wonder Woman has a 'cover': an everyday identity to hide behind when she's not fighting evil. As an ordinary mortal she's known as Diana Prince, and that's the way the world sees her until she's called on to change into the dark-haired goddess in the dazzling costume who can floor any enemy with the ease of a heavy-weight boxer!

Her origin

Wonder Woman was invented by an American psychologist, William Moulton Marston. He wanted to create a character that could be both human and superhuman at the same time. He once said, 'Wonder Woman saves her worst enemies and reforms their characters.' Wonder Woman made her first appearance in December 1941, just after America had entered the Second World War and she's been battling for good every since. In 1974 a very successful television series was launched starring Cathy Lee Crosby as Wonder Woman.

Zorro

'Zorro' is the Spanish word for 'a fox'. It is also the nickname chosen by one of the earliest heroes of the American west, a Spaniard named Don Diego Vega.

Vega lived in California in the 1820s, at a time when it was still ruled by the Spanish. His father was the governor and as a young man Diego was sent away to Madrid for his education. He was away from home for several years, and when he returned he found that his father had been thrown out of office and that a greedy tyrant had taken his place.

The real villain of the piece was the tyrant's military adviser, Captain Juan Rámon. Rámon was responsible for collecting the very heavy taxes from the people of the province, but in doing this he ruled the people with a rod of iron and took away many of their freedoms.

Diego hadn't been home long before he realised the tyranny under which his homeland had fallen. He decided that someone ought to defend the rights of the Californians and took it upon himself to free them from their oppressors.

Like the Scarlet Pimpernel, Diego Vega took on two different identities. As Don Diego Vega, the young man recently home from Spain, he gave everyone the impression that he was a weak pacifist. But as Zorro, the champion of the Californian people, he dressed in a black costume with a black mask and took on the governor's soldiers single-handed. Like Robin Hood, he stole back the money which Captain Rámon had collected in taxes from the people and returned it to them.

In the course of his adventures he won the secret love of the governor's daughter, but just to confuse matters she fell in love with Zorro, while rejecting Don Diego Vega, whom she regarded as a weakling. It was only quite late in the story that she realised that Diego and Zorro were one and the same man. In the meantime Captain Rámon had been trying to persuade the governor's daughter to marry *him* and the girl was torn between Zorro and the captain until finally the two men met in a duel and the captain discovered that he was *not* the finest swordsman in California!

His origin

Zorro was created by an American writer, Johnston McCulley who lived from 1883 to 1958. Zorro is his

best remembered character and has appeared in numerous films and television programmes since *The Mark of Zorro* was first filmed in 1920.

Post·A·Book

A Royal Mail service in association with the Book Marketing Council & The Booksellers Association.

Post-A-Book is a Post Office trademark.